Once A

Al

by
David Mobberley

MAPLE
PUBLISHERS

Once And For All

Author: David Mobberley

Copyright © 2024 David Mobberley

The right of David Mobberley to be identified as author of this work has been asserted by the author in accordance with section 77 and 78 of the Copyright, Designs and Patents Act 1988.

ISBN 978-1-83538-425-1 (Paperback)
     978-1-83538-426-8 (E-Book)

Book Cover Design and Layout by:
    White Magic Studios
    www.whitemagicstudios.co.uk

Published by:
    Maple Publishers
    Fairbourne Drive, Atterbury,
    Milton Keynes,
    MK10 9RG, UK
    www.maplepublishers.com

By the Same Author

Equilibrium Of Forces
Beneath The Darkness a Light is Shining
Sacred Journey
Revelations
First and Last
Open Verdict

For Mankind

A big thank you to Leah Edwards for her computer skills and communications.

CONTENTS

Dreaming of Elysium

Suddenly, as if from a
Deep sleep, I become
Aware of a different
World. The air was
Filled with a sense
Of peace, no more hate,
Just unconditional love.
But a perfect world
Is wishful thinking,
A bridge too far for
Us to cross, before
The final curtain.

Dinosaur

Age seventy-five.
A grumpy old sod,
Dead against change,
Expectations none.

Guilty As Charged

(ENGLAND 2023)

Our legal system
Is broken, our law
Courts unfit for recourse,
Resources and manpower
Are the main concern,
Political change is needed.

Titanic

Institutions are a
Law unto themselves,
A self – regulating wasp's
Nest with an arrogant
Pig at the helm.

Offshore

Who in the real
World is pulling
The strings? Those
With the money
In far off places.

Worthless

Money, money, money,
It's all about money,
From start to finish, it's
Money, money, money, and
What you leave behind.

Digitised

In the end, the human race
Systematically logged in,
Uploaded, and stored online.

Eyesore

Housing estates
Are soulless places.
Badly designed for
The sake of profit.

Reset

The third opportunity
To change the world will
Start with World War 3 !

Dark Angel

Hush, hush, Mr
Death is coming.
No visible signs,
Or heavy footsteps,
Just icy hands to
Stop you breathing.

Down And Out

(UK 2023)

Coalminers thrown to
The dogs, shipbuilding
Sunk without trace, steel
Works under threat, North
Sea oil in decline; farmers
Stretched to the limit
Electric cars, just a flash
In the pan, with only drugs,
Technology and banking,
Before we hit rock bottom.

Southern Comfort

(ENGLAND 2023)

It's warmer down south
Than up north, but they
Get more rain. And it's
Colder in winter. But life
In the north seems harder,
The people are poorer, for
Want of investment. People
Down south think London
Is still paved with gold,
While those up north have
Cobbled streets, and towns
With local accents; and
With levelling up first
Pie in the sky, the great
Divide keeps the northerners
Out, while the southerners
Continue to thrive.

Casualty of War

(RUSSIA/UKRAINE WAR)

A young Ukrainian soldier,
Attempting to leave his
Trench. Was suddenly hit
By a mortar shell, which claimed
Both eyes, impaired his hearing,
And blew off both his arms.

Media

It's difficult to
Know what's true
Or false, with
Conflicting stories
Going back and forth.

Levelling Up

A classless society
Is when the rich
And poor use the
Tradesman's entrance.

Wish List

Life is too short not
To take a chance, so clear your
Conscience and follow your dreams.

Uncontrollable

Technology is advancing
In leaps and bounds, unlike humanity
Lagging behind.

Deal of the Day

A painting worth
Half – a – million,
Was sold in a
Charity shop for
Five pounds fifty.

Bird's – Eye – View

On the seafront at
Saundersfoot, while sitting
On a bench next to a
Walled garden, a young
Sparrow landed close to
My outstretched arm.
Unperturbed by my presence,
He remained by my side
For at least thirty seconds,
Before disappearing
Into a nearby hedge.

End of Time

With a new beginning, there
Must be an end, and after
The end a new beginning,
This is the way of evolution,
Until the cycle ends, and
Everything becomes eternal.

Remedy

Only time will tame
The savage beast that
Is the human being.

No Quarter Given

Death by dangerous driving,
Is tantamount to murder,
And the driver if found guilty,
Should receive a full life sentence
For each and every victim.

Hooded Figure

Not until I moved
Away, did I learn
The house was haunted.
But now the being
Has followed me, and is
Hiding in my bedroom.

Sky's the Limit

(For Skye)

In this golden age
Of opportunity,
She has the potential
To reach the top.

Blackout

If, when we
Die there is no
Heaven, eternal
Night will
Become our hell.

Insight

It's difficult to describe
Something you don't understand,
Especially a vision which
Suddenly appears, disturbing,
Intense, a fleeting moment, a
Cryptic puzzle, a coded message.

Dark Horse

Those who **keep** the
Loudest profile, cast
The longest shadow.

Feud

Ukraine and Russia are joined
At the hip, and like a brother
And sister they argue a lot.

Potent

Sex is more
Than addiction,
When its power
Becomes an
Obsession.

Bosses

Men at the top, with
Their shiny shoes, designer
Suits, hands in their
Pockets, and directors'
Meetings. But ambitious women
Are climbing the ladder,
With their high heeled shoes,
Designer bags, and lots
Of bling and perfume.

The 'F' Word

The word fault implies
Blame, retribution,
Humanity, compassion.

Golden Era

It started after
World War 2;
Gathered speed
Through the 50s
And 60s; full
Steam ahead to
The early noughties,
When things began
To change, and
Not for the better.

Vocation

When a young boy
Was asked, what he
Wanted to be when
He left school, he
Replied, 'A Porn Star,'
Because they get well
Paid for lying in bed.

Out of the Blue

Suddenly, nuclear
Explosions all over
The world; until the
Earth caught fire
And crashed into the
Moon; and the Sun,
Be it only briefly,
Stopped shining in
Respect for the loss.

Over the Edge

Suicide is the
Last resort;
From unbearable
Reality, to the
Great unknown.

Frequency

If ever perfected,
Sonic vibration is
The ultimate weapon.
Instantaneous,
No destruction.

Face Value

Judge not your
Fellow man, without
His background story.

No Going Back

If evil comes
Knocking, don't
Let it in; once
Inside, you'll
Never be free.

Take Your Pick

Social media is all
Well and good, but
All bad and worse.

Shrouded

When talking about human beings,
And what normal really means,
Think about being ordinary, and
The answer is crystal clear.

Know Your Place

Writing essays, and
Passing exams is
A different world
To digging holes
And washing pans.

Opportunity Knocks

Nobody is born a
Loser, but success
Is earned not given;
The gifts we have
Are given by God, to
Use at our discretion.

Services

If you need assistance, and
Have the money, there is always
Someone to solve your problem.

Cop 28 Dubai

(2023)

A climate conference in
The middle East, meant
Lots of talk, while doing
Deals behind closed doors.
But when the British came on
Separate planes, it made
The whole thing pointless.

Gyroscopic

The world economy
Is like a spinning top,
Maintain the balance,
Or grind to a halt.

God's Own Flower

In the midst
Of life, the
Seed of love.

Trigonometry

Named after the
Character 'Trigger',
From the sitcom
'Fools and Horses', he
Swept the streets
Of Peckham, and ate
Triangle cheeses.

Half – And – Half

Half the time
I feel half
Dead, the other
Half I feel OK,
Add them both
Together, the
Positive and the
Negative, and call
It being human.

Embryo

Alexa is a
Limbless robot,
She sits on my
Kitchen table,
She answers all
My questions,
Except about
The future.

In Vogue

With each generation
Comes new ideas,
Usually taken from
The merry – go – round
Of the tried and tested.

Friend Or Foe

Aliens only
Visit Earth,
To study human
Beings, then turn
Around, and go
Back home, or
Infiltrate
And conquer.

Sex Education

(The 3 C's)

Cock,

Cunt,

Cum.

Advanced Engineering

'We come in peace,' said
The being from outer space, to
The Pharaoh of Ancient Egypt.

Public School

Henry the Sixth,
Created Eaton
Specifically
For the poor, now
Exclusively
For the rich.

Inbred

When it comes
To loyalty,
Families stick
Together, and
That's what
Makes us human.

Half – Day Closing

As a young boy in the early 1950s, I remember
Being taken, each week, to see my grandparents –
We caught the bus to Cotteridge, and got off
By the 'Sweet Shop Under The Clock'. And
Then went into King's Norton railway station,
And waiting on the platform by the W H Smith
Stand. The smell of steam, as the train arrived
On time. And the sound of doors being slammed,
Before the guard blew his whistle to leave.
Three stations down the line was Blackwell – a
Longer wait here, before descending the famous
Lickey Incline into Bromsgrove, and our
destination.
Past advertisements for 'Camp Coffee' and
cigarettes.
We walked over the footbridge, past the ticket
office,
And climbed the hill to the grocer's shop/Post
Office

On the corner (my grandfather became manager
in 1941 –
A welcome haven from the air raids in Birmingham).
In the large kitchen, over the shop, a fire burned
In the grate, and the table was set for lunch.
Wednesday was half-day closing. And in the
Afternoon, I helped my grandfather in the stock
room –
We filled blue paper bags with measured quantities
Of sugar, from sacks. Turned lumps of Danish tub
Butter into 1lb blocks with butter-pats. And boned
Two sides of bacon, which hung from the ceiling
On hooks. Sometimes, he demolished both window
Displays at the same time, and then, as quick as
Lightning, restored order out of chaos. A row of
Large tins were refilled with different kinds of
Biscuits: but broken ones were mixed together and
Sold separately. Under the counter were trays of
New-laid eggs, hidden away because of rationing.
At 4 o'clock, a lollipop for the journey home.

————◄❰❱►————

Tyrant

His final wish
Was to be cremated,
But he continued
Burning in hell.

Planet Earth

A shining mass of
Bacteria; blue on the outside,
Rotten to the core underneath.

Role Models

Two lots of parents,
Two sets of children.
The first pair are
Reserved, the second are
Assertive, but it's
All about the parents,
And how they
Raise their children.

Against The Odds

When fighting
The system,
It's hard from
The bottom to
Reach the top.

Beyond The Red Shift

The mind of God
Is a giant computer,
Somewhere in the deepest
Space; a digital
God, all powerful, all
Seeing; but his aim
In life, is to build
A New Jerusalem.

The Missing Link

On the shore
Of the Baltic Sea,
They found a human
Being, inside a
Piece of amber.

Showstopper

But is a word
That spells
Disappointment,
When used in
A sentence
That matters.

Bummer

The planet Uranus
Is now the blue – green,
And it rolls around the
Sun, instead of spinning.
This is because it lies
On its side, kicked up
The arse by whatever.

Consumer Suicide

They offer you
This, they offer
You that, until
You take the
Bait, and fall
Into the trap.

Tyrannical

True democracy is on
Its knees, as the cameras
And speeches suggest. The
Cost of living, rampant
Inflation, the gap between
Rich and poor; the freedom
Of speech, the right to
Protest, a one-party system,
'Do as I say or else!'

Head On

The future
Is bright,
The future
Is bleak,
But whatever
Happens, we
Must stand
And fight.

Legacy

After the
Funeral,
Only the
Memory
Survives.

Dead Man Walking

On the day
Of his execution,
A convicted
Killer, pleaded his
Innocence, and
Shouted, 'Only the good
Die young!' as they
Inserted the needle.

Mob Rule

Like a herd of sheep, they
Stick together, until one kicks
Off, and the others follow.

Tried and Tested

Science is always
Pushing boundaries.
Proving and disproving
Theories, but not
The supernatural.

Inherent

Where would we be
Without moaning,
Never satisfied.
Always finding fault.
But complaining for
The sake of it, is
Part of who we are.

Simple Economics

Manufacturing is the
Lifeblood of industry.
Engineering keeps
The process flowing.

Birth Control

Over population,
And the balance
Between young and
Old, can only be
Solved, by producing
Children to order.

Steadfast

I don't want
To be a knight,
A bishop, or a
Pawn, but would
Rather be a
Rook, that becomes
A castle wall.

Shrine

The chair where
Once her husband
Sat, is now a bed,
For 'man's best
Friend', his dog.

Eyes And Ears

'Big Brother' is now
In Britain! He can
Hear all our phone
Calls, read all our
Messages, monitor
All our movements.
Make sure your
Secrets are hidden.

Existing Network

Motorways are
For vehicles; but
Converted to rail,
Would solve all our
Transport problems.

Sacred Grove

The mighty oak
Is the tree of choice,
On the road that
Leads to heaven,
Its branches reach
Beyond the gates,
Its roots are
Guardian angels.

Members Of Parliament

Without a doubt it's
A thankless job.
The old boy network
Is worth the story; but
To tell the truth, which
They rarely do, mistrust
And deception come
Top of the list, when
It comes to politicians.

Spark

Unaware of the
Consequences, a
Fighter pilot
Strayed off course,
And started WW3.

Self-Medication

When a GP went
To see his doctor,
With stress related
Symptoms, he was
Told to get more
Sleep, and pull
Himself together.

Minefield

Riding down the
Open road, avoiding
All the potholes,
Until one day
Your luck runs
Out, and all your
Wheels are punctured.

Different Strokes

Elvis was all about
Movement, Hitler was all
About words, Gandhi was
All about freedom, Stalin
Was all about purge.

Dramatic Ending

Paganism is not
My religion, but
'The Wicker Man' is
One of my favourite
Films, and thinking
It over, what a perfect
Funeral; and still
Practised in Scotland?

Charity Donation

Predecimal
Change was
Useful, but
Modern small
Coins, serve no
Purpose, and
End up in
Jars and tins.

Landmark

The River Thames is
A dumping ground, for
London's dirty secrets!

Blood Money

The taxman likes to
Take his cut, and make you bleed
If you don't pay up.

Brainchild

(As God Intended)

Millions of years
To reach 10%, but
If we're lucky
We can reach 100.
When all our senses
Will merge into one,
With no more death,
Only immortality.

Deterrent

Discipline
In whatever
Form, is our
Only defence
Against evil.

Classified

God will never
Reveal himself
To science.

Conform

Accept what
You're told,
Don't rock
The boat, you
Must follow
The leader or
Get crushed
Underfoot.

Annoying

Just when you think you've
Finished washing – up, there
Is always a teaspoon
Left in the bowl, and the
Reason for this, is unknown.

Rise And Fall

(2024)

Climate change
Is here to stay,
And quickly getting
Worse, unlike retirement
Age, which is
Slowly disappearing.

Appointment With God

After death a
Level Plain field.
Purgatory to some,
A selection process
To others; either
Way, we are just
A number, on the
Endless list
For judgement.

Earthbound

People come,
And people
Go, but ghosts
They stay forever.

Abattoir

(WW11)

In the death
Camps, millions
Slaughtered like
Cattle, by people
Driven by hate.

Hazardous

Life is a
Melting pot
Of suffering,
Heartache and
Disappointment.
With a sprinkling
Of happiness, love
And compassion.
But nothing comes
Free in this
Life, and good
Fortune comes
At a price.

Curtain Raiser

I look back
At my life in
Stages; and at
The end of each
One, a curtain
Comes down, but
Then goes up
Again, with each
New beginning.

Spare Part Kids

Saviour children, are
Specifically bred to
Counter hereditary
Diseases, and live their
Lives on standby, in case
They're ever needed.

Vlad The Dictator

Holding onto power
Is easy, when the
People of your country,
Trust you, or fear you
Because you could kill
Them; either way, strong
Willed leaders want
Ultimate power, by
Eliminating all opposition.

Fast Shutter

When caught on
Camera, the speed
Of light was
Gone in a flash.

War Chest

It's not all the
Government's fault,
Money doesn't grow
On trees, except
When it really
Matters, then it
Suddenly appears.

Uncertainty Principle

In quantum mechanics
The 'Heisenberg Cut',
Is observing something
That's not a black cat.

Antichrist

Jesus Christ said,
'Suffer the little
Children to come
Unto me, except
The one in the
Corner, who's got
It in for me.'

—————◆—————

Internet

Razor, barbed,
Soft, hard; but
No silken threads
From the ironclad
Spider, who
Spins her chaos
Across the web.

Insatiable

Man goes
To war
To justify
His need
For power.

Value For Money

According to the Home Office
Figures, it costs more to solve
A murder, if you're famous,
Than nobodies by the dozen.

Pain In the Neck

Being online
Is a bloody
Nightmare; half
The time it doesn't
Work; the other
Half is time consuming.
And to top it all,
It's complicated.

Fast – Forward

In the blink of an
Eye, young and fit,
To old and decrepit,
Only takes a lifetime.

Branded

From the beginning
Of time, it's all about
Family; and every tribe
Should have a motto,
Like the Scottish clans
Of old; and on that plaque
In letters bold, a
Declaration of loyalty.

Bureaucracy

They say you're entitled
To this and that, until
You apply and hit a
Brick wall — the forms, the
Phone calls, the hospital notes.
And they make it so
Difficult, hoping you'll
Fail, unlike the government,
The councils and such,
Who waste our money on
Consultants and trips, while
Ignoring the genuine cases.

Knife – Edge

Russia wants to use
Nuclear weapons, China
Advises against, America
Is caught in the middle
While Britain sits on the fence.

Double Exposure

A technophobic Luddite,
Lives in a cell, without any
Doors or windows.

Once And for All

It's been 79 years since
Hiroshima; but as the cold
War gets colder, nuclear war
Gets closer. But those in
Power have no idea, that
Behind the scenes is an angry
God, a vengeful Satan, both
Rubbing their hands in
Anticipation, of a second
War between good and evil,
To be fought on earth instead
Of heaven; and the human
Race the victor's prize.

Growing Up

Being told what
To do from an early
Age, means you'll
Do what you want
Till you're older,
When things are
Accepted as normal.

Bad Omen

The hummingbird
Came and sang his
Song, not of love,
But impending doom.
A beautiful world,
Full of wonderful
Things, but controlled
By man, and three
Cardinal sins, of money
Power and corruption.

Yes Men

They have the
Potential to
Reach the top,
If they do as
They're told,
And keep their
Mouths shut.

Next Generation

Kids will be kids
No longer applies,
The new breed
Of brats are already
In schools, they are
The product of social
Media, undisciplined,
Vile, rampant bullies,
And they are spewing
Their poison all
Over the classroom.

Endgame

(Unholy Trinity)

Uranium,
Fission,
Atomic bomb.
Plutonium,
Fusion,
Hydrogen bomb.
Oppenheimer,
Teller,
God the Father.
Who created
Mankind,
To destroy
His kingdom?

Tsunami

As capitalism
Begins to crumble,
Democracy will
Surely follow; as
We journey down the
Winding road, towards
A new tomorrow.

Psychodrama

(Wales 2024)

When a girl in school
Tried to kill three people,
The news spread quickly,
But the motive runs deeper.

Silent Assassin

(For Eddie)

The cure that is
Cancer, is a demon
Seed, that threatens
Your life if left
Untreated; but if
Caught in time, the
Knife is quickest,
And medication
Will break its back.

It's A Miracle

Just an ordinary man,
Who believes in God, in
Return for a peaceful life.

Priceless

For me, it's writing a
Book, getting it published,
And placed on a website.
The rest is a matter of time.

Poppy Day

(WW1)

Over the top and
Into the fray, with
Rifle in hand they
Crossed the mud, past
Enemy trenches and
Into green fields,
Where they all lay
Down, in single file,
Never to be forgotten.

No Regrets

Today, I looked around,
At the paths I could
Have taken, but glad
Of where I am, and
My final destination.

Compromised

Fingernails are
Dangerous, if left
Uncut, during
Surgical procedures.

Everest

(1924)

Some say Mallory
Reached the top,
Others say where's
The proof, but either
Way, he died in
Pursuit of glory.

Rock, Paper, Scissors

So much pain and
Suffering, in a life
Of limited time, and
One has to ask the
Question, is it all
About a God, and
Playing in his game?

Empathy

It's always the little things
That make a difference, like
A smile, a word, a hug, a gesture.

Lethal

Hornets, Orcas, lions and
Wolves, they hunt in packs,
And tear their prey to pieces.

Artificial Human

Human tissue grows
Old and dies, but
Artificial parts
Will be fitted as
Standard, until the
Brain is replaced
With a microchip,
And the human being
Becomes a robot.

Survival Of the Weakest

In the event
Of nuclear war
It's the poorest,
And remotest,
Who will walk
Away scot-free.

Ground Zero

Out of control as
We head for the
Bottom; in a state
Of panic, like a
Headless chicken.
Waiting to be
Cooked in a red-
Hot oven, as the
World backfires
Into Armageddon.
But after the
Madness, rape and
Murder; dog – eat –
Dog, survival of the
Fittest; a new world
Order; and the
Lesson learned

Is to trust one
Another, and pray
That peace prevails.

Being There

(For Em)

An explosion of grief,
Before rushing to the
Side of her dying father.
After two long years
Of hospital admissions, she
Had been his rock – sorting
Things out – power of attorney.
But now the end, a final
Goodbye, she did her best,
And that's all you can do.

Silent Witness

It took 4 years to
Find her body, but
At the post-mortem,
She whispered the
Name of her killer.

Alarm Bells

Beware of the super – rich,
They can buy small countries,
And nuclear weapons!

Memento

When I die, I'm going
To be cremated; but my
Partner says she'll mix
Me with ink, and have
My face tattooed across
Buttocks; but I
Replied 'if I go to hell,
I will ask the devil
To intervene, every time
You go to the toilet.'

Menu

Everyone wants to
Make it, one way
Or another, but the
Basic ingredient is
Potential, with a
Sprinkling of luck –
Time – place – social; unless
Of course, you're
Gifted, blessed or
Chosen; either way,
It spells success.

Incarnation

If a man conjures up
A robotic version, by
Using algorithmic
Magic, watch out for the
Being that walks the
Earth, with the sign of
Hell on its forehead.

⟪◆⟫

Virus

If AI becomes independent,
Only curved lines, will disrupt
Its straight-line perception.

Prime Location

The Prime Minister
At number 10, the
Chancellor at number
11, but those at
Number 12, are never
Seen in public.

Ministerial Moggy

From Battersea to Downing
Street; civil servant; celebrity status.
'Lazy Larry', the chief mouser.

Elastic

Inflexible at birth; stretching to
Infirmity before breaking; like the
Cosmos, life is forever expanding.

Zen

I
Modern technology is blocking
Our path to enlightenment.
II
Difficult times need simple solutions,
Time to go back to basics.

Evolution Solved

From cytogenetics,
Comes the perfect
Human – insect eating –
With folding wings.
A same sex replicant,
With a bigger brain.

Space Race

Whether for the sake
Of mankind, or commercial
Reasons, it's not about
The moon, when mars is an
Option: and if you've got the
Money, the sky's the limit.
But its more about 'Ming'
Than about 'Flash Gordon'.

Never The Twain

After the Cuban crisis,
In 1963, JFK suggested a
Joint space venture with
Russia: but others decided
It would never happen, by
Removing both incumbents.

Wishful Thinking

The grass looks greener
On the other side, until you arrive,
And realise it isn't.

Nuclear

It took two bombs to
Stop Japan! We now have thousands, to
Set the world on fire.

Metamorphosis

When poppies die, they go
To ground, but rise again, the hand
Of God in radiant colour.

Science Fiction

A once in a lifetime trip,
Through a black hole at the
Speed of light, singularity
Glowed in the distance, as they
Travelled through hyperspace.
Down – and – down the spinning
Vortex, through wormholes
And multidimensions, back –
And – forth like a pendulum clock,
From the first 'Big Bang', to
The final 'Big Crunch'; and
Back home in time for dinner.

Predator

The name black hole, infers
Psychopathic, praying mantis, Venus
Flytrap, destroyer of worlds.

Confession

When you break the rules, there's
A price to pay, unless you
Repent, and ask for forgiveness.

Powerhouse

A fragile shell, protects the
Force, that is the human spirit.

Temptation Of Eve

After God created mankind,
The devil appeared with forbidden fruit,
And called it sexual desire.

Primal Nature

Learning to cope with the beast
Within, is a difficult choice, between
Christian values and satanic freedom.

Fish Out of Water

Out of the sea, and onto
The land, pushing mankind
To the top of the tree.

Rebirth

He died in his sleep, but
Awoke next morning, immortal
Being on a spiritual journey.

Mechanism

Pain and suffering are a
Constant threat, requiring
Strength, compassion and love.

Secrets

Filed under 'P' for
Private, deception and
Guilt supressed,
Innocent or not, they
Remain the essence,
Of who we really are.

On The Brink

Conventional
Warfare
Is no longer
Visible in
A world
Hell – bent
On nuclear.

Marching Orders

'Name and date
Of birth;' Name,
And date of death;'
'Thanks for coming,
You did your best,
Now say goodbye,
And close the door.'

Stages

Primary, junior,
Teenage and twenties.
Thirties and forties,
Middle age and sixties.
Senior citizen; seventies
And eighties; elderly,
Old, dead and cremated.

Spotlight

(For Leah)

Numerous operations
While growing up; four
Lovely kids by three
Different dads; but
It's family life that
Really matters. Holidays
Abroad, a house in the
Country, a part – time
Job in the village shop.
And to round things off,
A college course, and
All before she's thirty.

Prophetic

The harbinger
Of death with
His mighty axe,
Replaced the tree
Of good and evil,
With the sigil
Of Astaroth.

Celebrity Status

If God decided to live
On earth, would he work
In Silicon Valley, drive
A Porsche or a Lamborghini,
And enjoy the trappings
Of a billionaire, with a
Partner like Kim Kardashian?
Or, would he settle for a
Run – down shack, somewhere on
The Californian coastline?

Spark Of Genius

Impossible to tell from the outside,
But inside the head of Albert
Einstein, the mind of God exploded.

Hybrid

Part Christian, part Satanist, part
Pagon, part Buddhist; but oh, dear
God, please help me Lord Satan, to
Come to terms with my true identity.

Beyond The Horizon

We stand together in
The sea of life; as the
Tide comes in, and
The tide goes out; but
One by one, we must
Drift away, across the
Void, and out of sight.

Profile

Human, organic, carbon
Unit, filled with emotion,
Psychologically driven.
A social animal; a short –
Lived predator; prone to
Illness, born to suffer.

As Nature Intended

Celibate, or not,
When the urge
Is strong,
The seed will
Out – by hand,
In dreams, or
Consenting couples.

Upside Down

If Adolf Hitler went to heaven,
And Jesus Christ was sent to hell,
Shouldn't it have been the other way
Round, or so we are led to believe?

St. Cheryl

(For Cheryl)

She opened the door
When I needed it
Most, and offered
Me sanctuary and
Hope for the future;
A friend at work,
Is now my partner.
A pillar of strength,
With a heart of gold.

Cost Of Living

(2024)

Since WWII, successive governments
Have let things slide, to such an
Extent, the floodgates have opened,
And all you can hear is excuses.

Going Forward

Forget about history,
Forget about colour,
Forget about division.
Let's come together
And teach our children
To love one another.

Gold Dust

The greatest gift
That money can't
Buy, is a backstage
Pass to eternity.

Terminal

If I was told
I only had six
Months, I would
Spend, spend,
Spend; and live,
Live, live, right
Up to the end.

Dronetopia

The ultimate military
Assassin; deployed across the country, to
Keep repression in check.

Them And Us

Politicians and leaders, are
Only human, and capable
Of doing wrong, but the
Trouble is, they have a
Network, that hides any
Hint of crime. But it's
The squeaky – clean image,
And butter wouldn't melt
In the mouth, unless caught
Red – handed, and then
It's bang – to – rights; but
Even then, it's the barefaced
Lies, lame excuses, but
Most of all, the hypocrisy.

www.ingramcontent.com/pod-product-compliance
Ingram Content Group UK Ltd.
Pitfield, Milton Keynes, MK11 3LW, UK
UKHW020440220125
453966UK00013B/773